I Don't Know Yet
a collection of poems and prose

Alex Shea

This is for the Lights in my life.
Thank you for shining bright enough and long enough to give me time to root for myself.
I love you.

Intro

Every person in this world wants to be heard.
I'm not any different.

Sometimes I think things with the sole purpose of sharing them with somebody else, anybody else. I would rather shout into the void that is social media with my ideas than sit quietly and keep them to myself. There is too much available to all of us all of the time already.

What is one more voice?

I guess what I'm saying is— it was only a matter of time. I have dedicated an entire compilation to my uncertainty. My intention is not to rise in rank in this fame hierarchy. My intention is to share my ideas, to share a part of myself I don't usually get to set free, and hopefully start conversations— preferably with myself but if others be willing, you know?

I can honestly say I had no idea what direction I wanted to take my writing. I had no idea what I wanted to focus on or how I wanted to say it. I didn't know how comfortable I wanted to be when I put thoughts to word files. I was absolutely, positively confused and conflicted the entire time I spent creating this book and it was the best process I could have put myself through.

There were countless times I erased lines, deleted pages, and flat out tossed out entire projects because I felt they didn't fit the image I wanted to put out. Crazy— because, at the time, I didn't know what that image I was tossing entire projects out for was.

There were days I would wake up and lie there for who knows how long, asking my dog those pesky existential questions about what I was doing with my life— like any 20-something does... I hope.

Half of me hoped I had hopped into a reality where dogs could talk back and the better half of me knew nothing would come from me misdirecting my questions.

Even if my dog could talk, which sadly she's proven she cannot, she wouldn't have been able to answer my questions; I had to do that myself. There were things I continually put off talking about because of how young I am and how much I still haven't done and how irresponsible it would be of me to relate too soon, as a semi-broke college drop-out aspiring to be a writer.

But, I said fuck it. I might be young.
I might not know a hell of a lot.
But my eyes are my own.
And it would be my honor if you would let me share.

PART ONE

Hi you,

I want to start off by saying:
You can do this.
You've got this.
Say whatever you need.
Say whatever you mean.
Nothing is too much when you feel it in your gut.
Trust your gut.
Listen to your feelings.
They're so right.
All of the time.
I'll be checking in.

You can do this.

Release

In the middle of an empty parking lot, I'd stand
As rain poured, leaving trails down my skin
Embracing the heat releasing from within
Asking my inner truth to find a way out
There has to be something inside
Please, find a way around the lies
Sometimes the rain has the power to cleanse
In more ways than one, I'll admit
The letting go is easy when it's acceptable to submit
In a pool of water surrounding my feet
I release
For a moment or two before the sky swells up, I do

My happiest place would be that parking lot
Free, happy, without a trace of sin on me

Libra

I am not accustomed to saying no
I am overly aware of every yes that slips my lips
From the inner scale inside of me
Weighing the need to appease
With the nagging ideal to remain free
Losses and victories coincide
Become intertwined
Become the balance
Within the human I try to be

Butterfly

With every time I fell out of love with every role
I fell a little more in love with myself
I could feel myself becoming someone
I could feel my outer self connecting to my soul
Every position I ever held
Any part I ever played
Held no candle to the complexities
Waiting to be felt
There was no way I could ever find myself
When the only version I knew didn't like herself
Sick of falling out of love with my days
Tired of being anxious without a solution
Nobody should need to drug themselves to pacify
Any time the puzzle shifted in my favor
Another was in the cross-way
Versions upon versions of myself or them
Never mattered
As long as a me, that was me, came out in the end

Answers

She was so concerned
With what everyone else thought
And how everyone else felt
And what everyone else did
She kept losing her
For every time she ignored herself
A piece of who she was fell away
Until a silhouette began to take her place
Craving substance
Craving to be filled
Rid of the voids left by her own free will
She was not losing herself
For losing her way
She never had a way
To keep herself grounded
Forever, she had been running
Every way but her own
And it was becoming increasingly difficult to find hers
When she didn't know how
And the how was harder than the why
The why could be anything
Even the what was promising
The how was what had been throwing her off
Her entire life

Finally

For every word
That was never said
For every word
Said out of silence
I take them back
I take each one of those words back
They meant very little
Spoken from fear of discomfort
Rushed out from lips
Without expectation of being heard
I take my weary words back
For the chance to give you more
New words
Better words
Not out of silence
Out of woe
From someone capable of forming cohesive thoughts
Unhindered by embarrassment
Unconstrained by possibility
Each word will mean something
Not said just for sake of filling the space
Even my slip ups will be filled
With purpose, meaning

Soul Softener

I like doing laundry at my mom's house
Not for the obvious reason of it being free
Without a machine of my own
Even when I have my own machine
I still like doing laundry at my mom's house
Because when I get back
To wherever I'm staying at the moment
And I put on those clothes
I smell like home

Romantic Theory

If there ever was a time to ease my energy
I'd take that remedy with pursed lips
Nobody should ever confuse what it means to be lonely
Out of all the people I could have given attention
I chose the boy with the clouded heart
He was spreading himself too thin
He was tearing himself apart
I was unaware of the futility of my affection
My only concern had become falling in love
It didn't occur to me to stop and listen
The beating in your chest wasn't the same
When you saw my face as when I saw yours
For that alone, the beating in my own slowly waned

Unhealthy Coping

I think we're caught in this web
I've helped create
Wrapped up in who you could be
Instead of who you are

This isn't your fault
It's entirely mine
I take all the blame
For all the pride

I don't remember the last time
I saw you cry
Can't say I paid attention
To the reality unpainted by my mind

I feel myself die every time
I don't recognize those eyes
Or hear your words
Point out my lies

It is what it is
And it's not real
I made up our love story
With no account for what you would actually feel

Inhale Me, Exhale Us

If I can't make you feel something
If my touch does nothing for you
If my words don't make you high
If my energy has no affect
On what you're holding inside
I will understand
I am completely aware
Not everyone
Is meant for everyone
If I can't make you feel something
If my stories don't lighten your eyes
If my views don't challenge yours
If my presence doesn't make you weak
I hope somebody else can take your breath away
In a way I could never do

Unrecognizable

The closer I got to you
The further I drifted from me
The more I turned into
Who you wanted,
The more I turned into
A shell of who I used to be
Love
Unrecognizable

Out of Clay

Lying here, in the silence
Your eyes look up and down
As if I'm something to take in
Never take for granted
So I indulge in your stares
Tracing your lips with my eyes
Then my fingers
I take in how you look at me
Keep it in the back of my mind
Where I have learned to save
Memories like these

Lying here, in the dim light
Our fingers laced
As if they belong that way
Made to fill in the gaps
I keep track of the endless
Circles you trace on my palm
Then my knuckles
Trying to recall the last time
I let myself revel
In something other than nostalgia

Lying here, with you beside me
Hours pass
Minutes swept up in bundles
While we may be finite
Tonight
Tomorrow
These memories will be our relics
I'll keep mine
Like I always do
Just in case you forget yours
Like you're bound to do

But I know you, now
Like I knew him, then

Puddle

She is
In the rain
Literally
Figuratively
Metaphorically
She is
The rain

No

My body is mine
Please hear that
I might have forgotten
For those few moments
Feeling as if I had died
But I won't ever forget again
I know better
My body is mine
Please hear me
No amount of shame
Over that night
Will make me
Ever think otherwise

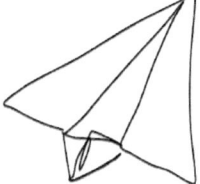

Hi you,

I told you I'd be back.
I just wanted to see how you were doing.
I see you're trying to group things.
Grouping your feelings as if that were possible.
You aren't being honest.
You feel in waves, not one emotion at a time.
Categorizing your experiences is hindering your expression.
Don't feel pressured to group to make this an easy read.
It isn't a How To.
This is poetry.
When has poetry ever been easy or for everyone?
It's okay to stop.
It's okay to keep going.
The empathetic need to release, too.
I'll check in soon.

You're doing great.

Alice

I wonder how common this place is
The space my mind created
I wonder how many other people
Have created this same space
A whole section of the inside, taped off
        Away from the lurkers and invaders
        Far away from any sense of reality
Entirely a creation of its own, in my head
Filled with love
The kind of love you don't run away from
    ...but run to
Lying awake at night picturing the most
Beautiful thing you've seen all day
    ...to feel it all in your space
A love that doesn't waver
Or ever entice
Engulfing itself until there's nowhere left
The happiness revealed is ever-present
    ...transforming itself as matter should
The kind of love pulling at strings
    ...connecting your heart to your tear ducts
Pouring the only form of emotion that you've
ever let yourself feel there—in that space
Everything is beautiful
Words make sense
Music plays without cue
The girl is twirled around as they dance
A beautiful house or apartment or dwelling of sorts
    ...is decorated wonderfully with their love for each other

Kissing and laughing and smiling
The air is pink because it can be
Nobody is hurt
There is no danger
The belief that love is truly out there
        And you can have that love
                ….is so fucking real, you can touch it
That space may be a creation of my mind's insane attempt
To love and be loved
But I wonder how common
And how often
The mind feels the need to create such a place
For you, too
           …not just me

I Choose Me

I realize I don't choose myself
I find it difficult to lose myself
I guess because I never found myself
I love the idea of every boy I ever meet
Because the one I truly ever cared about
Was a shot in the dark
                              And my aim hesitant
I realize I don't make it easy
I make a new thing die before it can grow
I guess it makes me feel in control
I like knowing I can shut it all down
Because start-ups are
Always easier than maintenance
I realize I begin again and again
I am accustomed to the loop I am in
I find the beginning to a chapter so charming
I guess the only reason you read is for the end
But I never get that far
I keep reading the first few lines
Over and over again
I realize I'm at a stand still
And the only way to move is to choose
I realize I never choose myself
I'm just hoping one day I might

Trap Door

There's no reason to
Lock
That
Door
Or to
Be
In
The
Dark
He knows
And you know
Nobody else
Even notices there's a door
There
In
The
First
Place
Sorry, baby

For What It's Worth

those bruises on my sides used to be visible. nobody saw them but me. i never let that happen. deep purple finger markings marking more than my skin. they used to sting at the touch of my own hands and the shower became a safe place. where the hotter the water was when it hit my skin the less compelled i was to scream at the top of my lungs. it's a good thing those bruises could be covered up with lies and t-shirts and somehow my memory considered you traumatic because it took so long for it to recover that lost year. shadows fell over that day and every day after that for a long time. over time the bruises faded, disappeared just like you and your family did out of my life. you were never meant to be there. i was never meant to be up that late. that door was never meant to be that heavy and useless. i see it in flashes now. never all at once. i used to blame you and myself and the bystanders because deep down I know they know and still do but i don't put blame on anyone. it was a dirty thing that happened and hopefully you're sorry by now. bruises may have vanished from my flesh but they will always linger in my subconscious. always kicking my ass. always telling me to make sure the water is hot enough. to wash away more than skin. nobody asked or is it that i never told. either. or. silent.

Self

How would you feel
If the only way you could be yourself
Was to strip away
Every trace of identity
Ever given to you
Up to this point

Unhinged

Do not minimize my situation
Do not put my pain in a deco box
Do not lock me inside
Tie a ribbon
Hide the key
My situation is real
No matter how often I escape
My pain is real
No matter how much I remember
My struggle with the truth is real
No matter how many times you ask
Nobody is making any of this up
Though I wish this were a satire with a purpose
It is not a story I would choose to tell
It is not a story I would choose to create
My abuse lasted a few moments
My pain has not gone away
Any mention contrary
        To my hesitant, wary admission
        After wearing guilt like a second skin
        That never quite fit, for years
Would be unsurprising
Yet not your place

Wave

Take the same amount of time
If not more
Engulfing yourself
In compliments
As you do
Drowning yourself
In insults

11 Sins

He took
And he took
My innocence
Punishing face
Calloused hands
He took
My piece of mind
He took
Greedily
Sure of himself
He took
My childhood memories
He took
The safety around me
Covered it in a filth
I still scrape off of me
He took
And he took
And he never apologized
And I never expected him to

Futile

I will never stop trying to wash away
The fingerprints that weren't mine
The breath that hit my skin
The sweat that reached my spine
The words that coiled themselves into knots
The whispers that stunted my childhood
The moment that left an infinite dark spot
No amount of washing I do will make my conscious clean
The years I spent laid awake at night
Skin raw, eyes red
Replaying
What I did, what I said
Why it happened so fast
Why it happened at all
Why I haven't said a word
Why I think washing it off
In every moment my skin hits water
Will make it go away
Will make me clean
Will lift the darkness
Coming out new
Eyes chapped, skin bare

No, Not Yet, Maybe

I'm learning that it's okay
To say no
To say not yet
To say I'm not ready
I'm trying to have the mindset
Without the guilt
After something sweet
Without the regret
After something harmless
I'm trying desperately to get my shit together
Jig-sawing my mind back together
To understand
That kiss
Is not this kiss
That hug
Is not like this hug
That if there is ever a time
I do not feel okay
I do not feel safe
I do not feel comfortable
I can say no without consequence
I can wait without fear of disappointing
It will always be a choice
My choice
I just have to use my voice

AA

Soaked through my gums
So this is what they meant
When they said one wasn't enough
Dripping down my tongue
To the back of my throat
The only memories are
Tied up and cloaked
By a composition so lovely
Don't mind me
I've been floating
With every intention of drowning

Introducing

Forgive me if my mind is never spoken
I've forgotten what truth tastes like
It has little to do with you
Everything to do with me
The words I'm thinking never make it out
Alive, free
The whole time I thought it couldn't be me
It's got to be the company I keep
How can that be true
All I do is shush myself away
Nothing is ever good enough to say
Break me free
Please, get me out of my head
To let everyone I meet, in

Momentum

Roads get blocked
By insecurities
Bad feelings
Unruly tantrums
Pride
Keep in mind
You'll never find
Your destination
Second guessing every turn
And always asking why

Hey you,

I'm happy you decided to stop grouping.
There were some tough bits in that last part.
They were the hardest to let out, I'm sure.
Remembering hasn't been easy for you.
But doesn't your heart feel lighter?
Don't you feel like dancing?
You are incredibly worthy.
I'm so proud of you for using your voice.
I'm so proud you're letting yourself heal.
Keep going.

I'll be here.

Serial No.

Everyone looks like everyone
And nobody looks like themselves
Trapped in this maze
We've created and coddled
Afraid to ever leave
Undeniably so, one day we will
Yet the structure of the maze holds comfort
When you never really know who you are

Existential

disconcerting
when it pulls out of focus
blurry as all hell
unsettling emotions
settling on the bottom
wherever that may be
confused and out of touch
losing grip on what
you thought your fingers touched
those aren't yours
none of this is
can't recall
whose reality this is
you just know
nobody really ever leaves
you never have

Cosmo

Acknowledge the dreams that you have
Accept the lessons they're trying to teach
Live accordingly
There doesn't have to be a mess
Nobody needs to fall into toxic habits
Pay attention to what your dreams are saying

Table for One

When we talk
We talk for one
We listen for one
We yell at each other
For one
Though nobody hears a thing
We call it conversation

Eat

That pit in your stomach is alive
Wanting the bodies and minds
Of everything it does not have
Of everyone it has not met
In your defense
You might have thought your mind
Did all your thinking for you
Until you felt that hunger
Until that hunger began to consume you
It never goes away, not really
It lingers
Whether you ignore it
Whether you indulge it
Lives, yours and theirs
Are at the mercy of this insatiable beast

Woman Girl

I did love her once
Before the lust
Before the loss
Before she forgot who she was
I coddled the worst of her
To try reaching the best of her
Foolishly, it seems
She is no longer the girl I loved
She became a woman
One I fear and admire
Simultaneously
As a woman is meant to be

Role Models

I will reference every movie I need to
Until you see between the lines
You realize that my words are just their words in disguise
With each one of my renditions
Every last impression
Sometimes my own feelings cannot be explained
Without the help of someone else's
Hopefully you see that
Hopefully you see me
In the films I have you watch
In books of mine you read
There's a part of you
That comes a little closer
To the light inside of me
The hidden channels
The mystery I hide beneath

E for Empath

Trade with me for a day
Just the one day
Be the one that feels everything
All the time
Just for one day
That's all it'll take
Then tell me you wonder
Why I cry sometimes
In a room full of people not saying a thing
Why I smile sometimes
At someone that barely looks my way
Why I laugh out loud
To the jokes I tell myself
Why my eyes fill with tears
After a good story, a good movie, a good song
Happy or sad
I feel it all
Trade with me for a day
Feel your days the way I feel mine
Then ask me why
I still believe in a beautiful life

Whistle Blower

Screaming
In a room full of voices
Telling me
To hush
Screaming
So they hear me this time
I cannot be
I will not be
A miracle
To witness
Screaming
So they understand
My lungs will give out at any time
If they continue to neglect me

Bubble Wrap

Who could've thought
Laying yourself out
In an abundance of pages
Of memories
Of unspoken thoughts
Of realizations
All of them
Safely wrapping around you
Would be so deafening to the outside

Pauvre

The only hand I'd like to hold
Is that of little girl me
Who hasn't gotten the worst of it
She has no worries
She has yet to tell herself to forget
Or make herself remember
She has everything
She could ever ask for
Because she has never had to ask
For anything else
Maybe if I could hold her hand
Walk her through
What hasn't happened
She wouldn't be so afraid
To hold
The hands of others

Mr. Universe

somehow this might be a surprise but I was hoping you could change it all somehow making everything fit together into the puzzle the universe intended. somehow allowing me to heal inside simultaneously with changing the way I see the world outside. somehow you were the one I needed in the midst of everyone else I had as if somehow you were the one saving me from what I had no control over. somehow I might not have realized that you were only ever meant to be you, not mine. there was something about the way you never finished sentences and paused for me to fill in the blanks. there was a whole reality within those sparkling eyes of yours, that I now realize were emptier than they led on, as if the future was something you personally wrote with a pen right before you went to bed. there was something childish about the way you pretended to depend on me to make up your mind when I knew damn well you already knew what our lives would end up like. how did you know and when did you write it out and why didn't you take me with you?

Content

For once it could be easy
Falling asleep comfortably
To the sound of a happy heart
That belongs to me

dtr

When you're sure of me
Don't tell me right away
Let me linger, anticipate
Make me wait for a sure answer
Nobody likes to really know
All the fun is in the mystery
The maybe of it maybe happening
Not the actual actualities in between

World-Crossed

i'd like to dance with you
even if you say you don't know how
even if you really don't
i'd like to dance with you
i'd like for you to be comfortable with me
i'd like to meet you first
then dance
for hours
as if i had known you all this time
and we just needed to dance to remember

The Poet

Love me deeply
You don't need to be afraid
Not of me
Love me as long as you can
I understand hearts
Have a temperament
I won't mind a bit
And when you're done
With me
Tears have fallen
Souls are worn out

That love will live
In my words
On paper or in a file
Somewhere I'll experience
That type of exhaustion
Again and again

Stuck Behind

For every hand I never held for
fear of forgetting where mine
was, I'm sorry for never
letting myself get lost in your
touch. I was only thinking of
every touch I lost myself in
and never truly came out of.

Single Syndrome

I don't want to hold you
Don't ask me why
When I'll change my mind
I decided in this moment
While you were looking into my eyes
That intense stare, soft and pure
I could see you needed me
More than I could reciprocate
Don't feel sorry for me
Patronize my limitation
Oh, why can't she
Understand
I can't give you the amount of me
You might believe
Wish of me
I know me better
Estranged, maybe
Relax your expectations
I don't want to hold you
Not yet
Later, maybe
Maybe not at all

Growing Pains

I've never wanted anybody
I was never wired to want
The traditional way
Getting older
It hurts
When I want to want somebody
But everything inside of me is screaming
I won't know what to do
With what I'm given

Whim

No I didn't mean to
There was nothing that I said
That wasn't what I meant
At the time
There was nothing that I did
That wasn't how I felt
At the time
But life happens and I changed
So did my words
So did my actions
I thought it was okay
To change my mind
Still I didn't mean to
Hurt your ego
Wound your pride
Break your heart
I wanted to make a nonexistent
Relationship fly
That was my mistake
I never learned when to stop
Playing pretend
I still haven't
I do apologize
But know I didn't mean to

Yo-Yo

Those things I do to you
Are things that were done to me
It's possible they had no clue
I myself took a while to see
Feeling with the fervor of the sea
Crashing onto the shore
Pulling you in, pushing you back out
Unaware of the hurt I leave
Of how toxic I can be

Snake

There were turns in his words
That cannot be explained
Like the way a record skips
Sometimes, when it plays
Without an air of error
Such a whirlwind affect his words had
On everyone who had the pleasure
Including myself
The one giving him
Speech lessons

Roofies

You press your lips against my neck
And tell me I'm in ecstasy
It's no wonder you press against so many
When you force the pleasure
You undoubtedly believe you're creating

Permission

I'm in love with a boy
Who has no idea
And I will love this boy
While he has no idea
Because that's the best way
The only way
I know how to love someone else
With no chance of ever getting said love in return
My heart works more efficiently this way
Overindulging in romance
Never expecting romance back
Complacence
No it is not the unrequited
That I fear
It is the brave
That try and love me in return
Or without my knowledge
That terrify me
I've never had the pleasure
Of a mutual love

Lusty Gal

Forever longing for the looks
From the ones forever looking
At somebody else

For the Boy

I can't remember your middle name
For the life of me I can't remember your middle name
It's a shame because the rest of your name is another man's name
and another man's name all the same
The one thing that could separate you is your middle name
And I forgot it
It's possible I never asked
Because quite frankly I never cared
Not at the time
You were you and that was all you would ever be to me
I know you may not have understood and looking back
I'm having a rough time defending myself
I saw you but I never saw you
But you, you saw me
Not right through me like everybody else
You saw inside of me
You carved at my insides like there was treasure to be found
I'm sorry all you found was me
You saw me the way I didn't even see myself, not yet
If you could have seen the way you looked at me
Boy how you looked at me
It could make a fire beg for refuge
Now I'm not trying to say I'm sorry for being me at the time
Or that I'm ashamed of who I was because I'm not either
I was who I was for a reason and I am who I am because of it
What I'm saying
Is that all that time you spent looking at me, learning me
I was trivializing you
Nothing was meant to be taken out of context

But everything was
If I had looked at you with half the intent with which you looked at me
I would've seen it
What I'm saying
Is that you looked at me like your life depended on it
and I never bothered to learn your middle name

bts

Nothing makes more sense
Than proclaiming your love
For someone who forgot you exist

twntys

My bed isn't the same without
Regret lying by my side
And it sure as hell feels empty
Without a body
With mixed emotions for me beside

I can't decide what's worse
Being alone with guilt
From the last morning
Or being alone with anxiety
About the next

Surely my bed can be happy again
This time
With a more capable host
Finding a bedside companion
More intent on fixing the bed
In the morning
Than rummaging for spare pieces
On the way out

I can't tell what's better
Hoping for a day
I wake up to escape my dreams
Or hoping for a day
I won't be able to sleep
If I'm by myself
Ever again

Weary Flower

The outline of her body
Dipped and curved and carved out
Adventure
Craving to be touched
Wary of the commitment
Begging to be held
Cautious of who held her
Sure that someone better
Would come along and forget her

Tender Thumb

Saying you miss someone
You haven't seen in a while
Might not even recognize
Is like saying you can't help a flower grow,
Blossom like it should
Without a hose
Yet an endless supply of rain

Dreamy Eyes

I am not the me
You thought I was
And I'm not sorry
For being the me
I dreamt for so long
To meet

Not Myself

The trembling begins
Subtle at first, then all over
It's not the trembling
That gets me
It's the miscommunication
Of when and where the trembles go
And how long they last
And how I never know
I was never very good at control
The concept of it
The trembles took what little I did manage
I can no longer tell my body what to do
Any more than I can tell yours
I'm not sad
I'm not mad
I'm in between
This delicate state
Where I understand
Where I cope with pain
These trembles I live with
These trembles I feel for
These trembles are mine

Loose Limbs

Until you've felt your body give up on itself
Somehow depending more on itself
With a sudden need to create a coalition of limbs
Until you've grown numb
In places you once experienced touch
Pinching yourself on good days
So you can never forget how a pinch feels
Until you've received that unwarranted honor
Hosting limbs that do not obey
Hesitantly entrusting your body with involuntary motions
Until you've been told
It's all in your head
The pain is faux
The walls aren't white
There's just no way a limb can commit
Such horrid acts you claim
Without proof
A thread that shows you're unraveling
Until you've adjusted and recognized
There are times your mind and your body will not coincide
Sometimes that is life
Sometimes that life is yours
That, that life, is fine

Until then
Anger will bubble
Sadness will follow
But after
You will be you again

Not Enough

There's something about a time limit
Makes everything a little more urgent
A little more important
There's only so much time before
Time is up
That really does something to a person
Who never thought time would run out
Give up on them

Fear Billfold

It never truly leaves you, does it?
That fear is always underneath
You never get over it, do you?
That fear has seeped through
You've learned to live with it, haven't you?
It's become a side effect you stopped questioning
It still creeps up on you, doesn't it?
When you start to believe you could be fine
It has become more than fear, hasn't it?
That fear has become you

It's a lot to carry, isn't it?
Never knowing when you can breathe
It can get weary, can't it?
You know you can't always be right
Then how is it
Your heart skips five beats
When everything is going just fine?

Simon Says

I never had to think about my movements before
Each one now so intentional, so precise
My mind wants to remember days when my body could
For days when my body cannot
Once in a while I think of before twenty
When I was clueless to the illusion of power
Right before the pen slipped from my fingers
In the same instant the frivolity of control
Imprinted itself in my mind

Episode

My chest has been on fire for hours
Fireworks setting off in unison
With one phone call
Five more for good measure
A clenched fist around my heart that keeps squeezing
There is no longer a ransom
For what it has destroyed
Just clumsy knuckles scraping a hollow chest
With each voice calling to soothe me
I hope for release, more give than take
But their words encourage that fist
Twisting and pulverizing
Good to know what I counted on more than anything
The life source within me
Would leave my vessel with a wounded spirit
A broken frame, gasping for air
As I try to remember why I laid my head
In my shaky hands, in the first place
Saturated in sadness or pain or both
Knowing my chest will never be okay again
At least never the same
That sadness covers every inch of a heart
That has lost too many times
No, I don't believe these fireworks will ever disappear
They may dull themselves over time
But for now, they serve a purpose
My naivety is in need of a lesson
These fiery sensations will teach
Before fading into remission

Hi again,

I can see you're working through some things.
Pretty selfish.
I know it might seem messy and out of sorts.
So okay.
It's all coming out beautifully.
Maybe talk about more than you.
You're a part of a million other lives going on.
A million other things.
Either way, keep talking.
Your heart is warming.

Garden of Apology

For every flower that's never bloomed
I say,

I apologize for all the days you spent hoping
Every chance for flourishing mistaken
Yearning for the sunshine in a field of shade
Patiently awaiting your potential

I apologize for the weeds you never recognized
Catching only glimpses of the leaves beneath you
Turning brown despite your efforts to grow

I apologize you never saw the shine you needed
For the rain that escaped you
It is not your fault you never thrived
Never bloomed

You tried
Anyone can see that
From the tribulation
The fight against the wilt you put up

Miseducation

Maybe it's not how much
I loved you
But the only way I knew how
That ruined us both

8 Ball

All of these questions
Without real answers
They keep pouring out of me
Some things don't have answers
Some things just are
I'm in no condition to decide
My entire life
With each blink of my eye
Not when it took me years
To find my curiosity
Underneath my once passive mind

Momma

Epitome of strength
Mother of mine
Rooting yourself
In sorry soil
To nurture your branches
As they grow leaves of their own
Making sure they don't fall
Futilely
Strength in solitude
You've shown me
The right has as much right
To feel wrong
Flowers don't need complete sunlight
To grow
Strength in possibility
Never truly knowing your own fortune
Yet taking a risk on everyone else's
You are it
Mother
You are everything
Embodying strength
So much so
You've become it

Delete

How could you ever think
Leaving this world would make it better
When you are the world
To so many others
How can you say you are being selfless
When your reasoning revolves around you
More than less
How could you ever think
You mean nothing to everyone
When you mean everything
To at least one someone
Please don't think of going away
Care enough to respect your timeline
If you're not there yet, you will be
If you're not happy yet, you will be
If you're not sure yet, you will be
Please just hold on

First Impressions

Do I want to be you
Or be with you
When infatuation creeps
I lose a night's worth of sleep
Is it you I want to appear next to me
Or a better me
A me someone like you would need, too

Blended

Little girl with the curls falling around her waist
A momma with waves in her hair
Happiness in her teeth
Skin the color of sand
A poppa with a voice meant to tell stories
Lightness in his step
Skin the color of coffee
They do not know
The consequences their love had on you
You were made out of love
In a place that saw it strange
You were raised to be loved
In a place still ashamed
Your momma and poppa thought it ended with them
But they were wrong
So wrong
You were the beginning
Not the end

Wilting

You speak loudly
Never once about much
You've grown accustom
To sharing irrelevancies, dislikes you have
In the world
With me
You fail to notice
I cannot do much
I do not care much
Anymore, anyway

You speak loudly
Full of anger
Full of self doubt
I want to share with you
Tools filled with light
So you are better able
To share the good in the world
With me, instead

And I can finally listen
Welcoming a once dreaded presence

But you seem to drown
Every seed
I plant in exchange for your pain

Tous les Femmes

I will not apologize
For somehow always being undermined
My charm compromised
By my body

I will not apologize
It is not my fault
Nor my responsibility
To provide a guideline

I will not think for others
While the debate on what is harmless goes on
You either know or you don't care

Look Around

My eyes are always in the mood
To cry
They don't know the difference
Between a thing
It's all so beautiful
It's all so sad
They're just here
Constantly betraying the reason in my head

The Sun

Sometimes I stare at the sun and recite an array of compliments to it. I tell her how magnificent she is. Yes, she's a she. She has the power to create life and end life. She is a she. Thank you. I tell her how magnificent she is. I tell her how amazing her warmth is. I tell her how unworthy we are as a species to live on a planet orbiting her. Sometimes I stare for so long I get overly emotional and I tear up. She doesn't mean for me to cry. She cannot help but to be so complete. I gaze at the sun as if she were gazing back at me. I stare at the sun out of amazement. She is so beautiful. She is so powerful. She is so magnificent.

Buried

There's so much more to life
Than what you find wrong with it
Where have you been looking
For so long
You see only darkness now
How long
Before you see the light again
How many cracks do you need to create
Before light finds its way back to you

Dad

Place that arm around me
Spin me around
So gallantly
Watch for my toes
But laugh when I step on yours
Twirl me
Like the little girl I am
What I wouldn't give
To sway with you again
Even if it's to that sweet melody
I made up
Only ever playing inside my head

Swallow

Miles cannot ruin a relationship
All of those tragedies
About long distance
Are told by people who believe
The love for someone fades
With every mile in between
Miles are not what ruin a relationship
Miles do not weaken a connection
The temperamental do

Bring Me Home

We were kids
We didn't know about anything
We played and joked and got along fine
Time went by
I forgot who you were
Vaguely
I forgot your face, not your heart

We were teenagers
We knew something about some things
We talked about everything and became close
Time went by
I forgot who you were
Vaguely
I forgot your face, not your heart

We were a little older
We knew what we felt
We never said it out loud
We knew the truth
Time went by
I forgot who you were
Vaguely
I forgot to call, but not to think of you

We are adults
We know more than we did
More than we should

Feelings have vanished
Vaguely
You forgot about me
Completely
You're in someone else's arms now
But I remember you
Completely
You bring me home

Mobile

Always in a rush
Just to get to a table
Reserved for one
In a room full of other people in a hurry
Just to get to another meeting
In a room full of other people in a hurry
Just to make it to their train
To make it home, empty
To make the phone call, to nobody who has time
Nobody has time
To sleep in a bed, alone
Everyone is always somewhere else, important
Always in a rush
Forgetting to remember to slow down
You could be missing what is happening now
By worrying about missing what hasn't happened yet

Glass Ceiling

the ugliest thing
a woman can do
is create
imaginary rules

> (for fear of her past)
> (for fear of living her present)
> (for fear of creating her future)

to live her life to

With Thorns

She's so pretty
For a girl
Who can't accept herself
As a woman
Keeping herself
At a distance
From happiness in all its forms
Ignoring the nature
Of most of the world
To keep a strong grip
On the girl
Who never could believe in herself
But boy, is she pretty

Match

Girlishly on fire
Her body in flames again
Like only a girl can understand
Unlike any man who has chosen
To stand before her, beside her
Inside her
Agony is a mistress all her own
Better handled in tangled sheets
She does not cry
She does not scream in pain
She internalizes her externalities
A skill inherited through intuition
She reaches her climax
Then comes back down
More secure than ever
The mistress likes to keep the sheets warm
Ensuring a cozy return
She herself can admit
She would miss affirmation after affirmation
Of the strength her body holds
Through to her inner self
The threshold this kind of strength creates
For any embodiment of negativity the world fabricates

Wholesome

I miss my family
In a wholesome way
In a
Want a hug, not need a need a hug, way
In a
Face to face conversation
More than a small talk
Keep those eyes on me way
In a
My heart aches when I don't see them for days
Or hear their voices often enough way
In a
Laughing till my face creases
Comfortable as ever, not to fend off awkwardness way
In a
Gossip with my ears
Not my mouth way
In a
Desire to know what their movements are every day way
If they're being safe
In all respects
In a
Desire to hear their eyes
Because I still can
I miss my family each minute of every day
I'm not around them
That does not mean I hover
That does not mean I have no life of my own
I do

I am living quite well
I miss my family mostly
When they are around me
Talking in my face about nothing
Smiling to each other in my presence
I watch the family I miss
Intently, carefully
To appreciate how good I have it
To appreciate how deeply I'll miss them
When I cannot watch them anymore

PART TWO

Spilled Tea

The other day I was sitting in a coffee shop and I ordered tea.
Unusually so.
To make things even more foreign, they brought it out teapot and teacup.
I was meant to pour my own cup of tea.
Which should have been fine.
Honestly, I shouldn't have had any issues.
I've poured tea before.
Something about this teapot, no—everything about this teapot wanted to keep me from achieving a cup of tea.
Hesitant and unsure of what exactly I was doing, the tea kept spilling along the sides, creating puddles of perfectly good tea.
What was I doing wrong?
I knew how to pour tea, I thought.
The only difference between me at home and me in a coffee shop was the hesitation I felt.
Oh, and the coffee shop full of patrons watching the idiot spill tea all over the place.
I chose to focus on hesitation.
That had to be the real key.
Hesitation had to be the reason I couldn't complete such an easy task.
Hesitation had to be the reason tea kept pooling around the teapot instead of landing in my teacup.
I didn't expect a life lesson from my teapot, but I welcomed it.
Hesitation leads to unserved tea which then turns cold which then defeats the purpose of ordering hot tea on a cold day.
In the same way hesitation prevents progress which then turns to regrets which then turns into fear.
Such a life lesson doesn't just spring out of a simple cup of tea.

I had to have been looking for it.
And I found it.
And poured the damn tea with at-home confidence.
And drank a nice cup of hot Earl Grey.
And maybe there was too much confidence.
Hence, drenching my pants as well.

Talk 2 U

The average person's need to feel appreciated is overwhelming and in most cases, unappreciated.
It all falls back to how we are terrible at communicating.
All of us.
All people.
We are terrible communicators until we acknowledge our shortcomings and work to correct them.
Which only a few of us do, for sake of what?
Pride? Ego?
Whatever it is holding us back as a society from learning how to communicate without the curve of small talk, let's please find it- diagnose it- eradicate it.
Too many times we have misunderstood or misinterpreted a situation solely because we didn't ask that question, didn't answer that question, ignored that gut feeling.
No more.
If speech is a freedom, I want to indulge.
I want to bask in my freedom.
I don't want to talk about things I don't want to.
I want answers to the questions I ask.
I want to answer any and every question I possibly can.
I want to hear stories people have found unworthy of telling.
Those are the jewels.
Whatever makes your eyes light up is what you should talk about.
What everyone should talk about.
Make everyone else's eyes light up, too.

Wall Theory

I accidentally scribbled on the wall today.
Just a single line, sprawled along the grooves that made up the wall in my bedroom.
It wasn't a terrible mess.
It wasn't anything spectacular to look at.
Just a fine line running across a creamy wall.
Something done when I wasn't paying attention, probably writing something somewhere, mid-thought, pen in the air.
Like anyone in this situation— or maybe anyone in this situation...
How many people are out there accidentally scribbling on walls these days that aren't in their terrible two's?
Like anyone in this situation, I tried erasing the mistake.
Mistakenly so.
The tiny scribble on the wall became something much worse.
It was no longer a clean line against a rugged canvas.
Ink, smudged now in places and sinking into the wall.
Maybe nobody would have noticed the line on the wall before, but now they absolutely would.
When I attempted to fix the line, it rebelled.
Throwing some sort of temper-tantrum only irreversible objects know how to throw.
As if to say, "yes you made me, but a mistake is not what I am—what I am now is just an addition to this wall."
I can't argue with ink.
I also can't fix everything.
Because not everything needs to be fixed.
My impulse to correct something I had no control over, something already in existence, was ineffective.
That isn't to say I will never try to correct myself again.
I just know better than to dismiss the nature of circumstance.

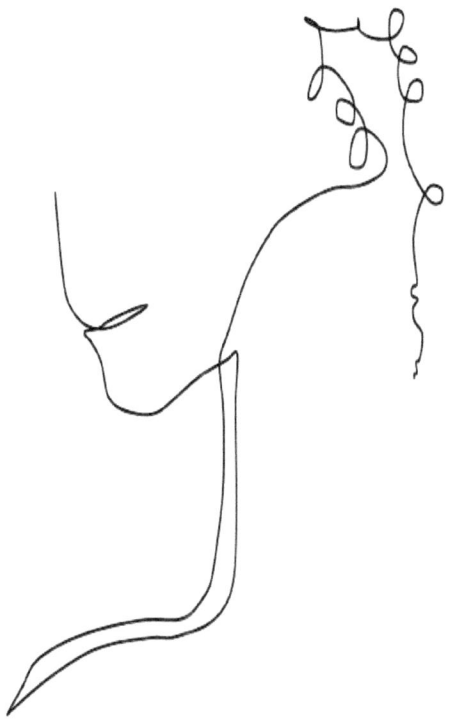

Femme/Femme

If I had enough courage to stand on my own two feet like plenty of women before me, I would take the world by storm.
Not to say I don't hold a courage all my own, but it doesn't suffice for the radical change I feel in my bones.
Using a craft of my choosing and a view from my eyes to change the world's mind about—
The way I was born and the anatomy I was given.
Followed by labels I was stricken with, but looked at from an onlooker as labels I was blessed with.
Either way, I'm not buying what's being sold.
Either way, I'd much rather use my ideas than those ideals.
Being a person is about so much more than a blanket or a name given to us by another.
Those of which are based primarily on societal shame.
Then there are efforts meant to lift shame and recognize a familiarity amongst one another.
But would there be one without the other?
A lot of effort, you see, is put into making someone a person all the same.
We all breathe and live and dream.
Unfortunately, not all wholeheartedly.
Like a dreamer, like me, would like to believe.
Many of us are clouded.
Disrupted by our differences.
Our thoughts and opinions and our beliefs have become these ceilings to box us.
Rather than starting lines to guide us.
I would like to show my appreciation for women before me.
The ones who ignored those ceilings.

And the ones who refused to sit quietly in a box while their surroundings were built by standards and locks.
I would like to acknowledge women from every generation.
For speaking up and holding ignorance accountable.
In a society where being quiet for the sake of consistency
Was, has been, and still is a preferred consolation.

Fool

Where are your eyes?
Never taking behold of what's in front of you because you assume it'll always be there.
Of course, it could be.
But then again, it probably won't.
Where is your heart?
Never daring to say how you feel because you chalk it up to having time to later.
Nobody ever says when later is.
Or how late is too late.
We need these measurements.
Where do you keep your wonder?
Always forgetting to watch the beauty in the way two people look at each other because you don't have the time.
Your destination must be of the most importance.
Ignoring life's small moments this way.
Not every moment is made for you and that's okay.
Enjoying moments in another world is nice, sometimes, too.
Where is your fire?
Always ignoring the way your insides light up when you're touched because you believe it all ends the same.
Where have you been?
You won't even think about accepting yourself because you're so sure nobody else ever will.
Are you alone or are you lonely?
We were never supposed to feel both simultaneously.
Are you happy or are you content?
We allow ourselves what we feel we deserve.
You have no idea of the person you can be outside of what everyone else sees.

Be a fool.
For you.
For me.
Stop and stare in adoration at every display of affection.
Not everyone expresses so openly.
Indulge in each caress, platonic or otherwise.
Tenderness is not given as easily as it could be.
Say what you feel when you feel it and even feel it after.
Feel.
Please, I beg of you, feel.
The highs are far higher than any low.
So. Feel.

Yellow Light Stance

Going forty miles an hour behind a blue Honda.
Or maybe it was something else.
Cars confuse me; I have no idea what kind of car it was.
Forty miles and a green light turns yellow right as the car in front of me gets to it.
Naturally, if I was faced with that yellow light, I would have driven right through it.
Not gone faster.
Not slowed down.
Definitely not have stopped.
But this blue ambiguous car stops even though there's enough time for them, me, and maybe two cars after me to make it through.
Given I had the time to think about this.
I had the time to weigh out my disappointment, too.
Why was I angry when this happened?
Why was I disappointed when somebody didn't react to a yellow light in the same way I would?
And I came up with our individual assessment of risk.
That's all a yellow light is.
Maybe driving as a whole is about risk, but for the sake of my sanity and this single car ride I was evaluating the meaning of a yellow light.
What we do with a yellow light says a deal about us, I think.
Whether we ride it out or halt.
Whether we speed up or slow down.
Honestly, even our reaction to the car in front of us when faced with a yellow light says something.
I came up with the conclusion that I respect risk.

The idea of it.
The follow through of it.
The consequences of it, even.
In regards to respecting risk, I have a tough time understanding why others don't when they are presented with the opportunity to.
I'm only upset for a few seconds but a few seconds of something like this is enough to frighten me.
I like risk.
Yes.
But at the sake of my peace?
Nah.
What do you do with a yellow light?

Runneth Over

At my day job I watched as the cook filled bowls.
Three bowls to be filled with spinach from a large pot.
The spinach isn't important.
The bowls are.
He had three— the same size.
What caught my attention was how he filled them.
The first bowl was filled with just the right amount.
With the other two in mind, but filled.
The second bowl was filled with the last in mind.
To make sure all three had roughly the same amount inside, I suppose.
In order to make sure the third bowl was filled properly, the second bowl was slightly less filled than the first bowl.
Interesting, sure.
Bear with me.
Now the third bowl.
The third bowl was filled with only the intention of being filled adequately in mind.
It was filled in the same way the first had been filled.
With a comfortable amount.
But there was still spinach left in the pot.
Not much, but some.
I watched as the cook put the remaining bits into the second bowl.
Though in the end the second bowl wasn't as filled as the first or third bowl, it was closer than before.
This entire thing made me think of my two brothers.
Our relationship in regards to one another.
Our dynamic in our family.
What it must be like to be the middle child.

How it felt to be the first born.
Because that's what I was.
All of the initial love thrown your way.
All of that love slowly waning to cover your siblings.
I never truly understood why there was such a thing as middle child syndrome.
But watching the cook as he filled the bowls that day, I understood a little better.

Hello?

Ever get to asking yourself, why?
Why do everyone else's lives interest you so much?
More even than your own.
We try to live vicariously through anyone else.
Why do we depend so heavily on seeing other people succeed?
In order to feel like we're able to.
Like there wasn't a reason to grow until they did.
Why do we invest ourselves in the livelihoods of strangers?
Picking sides, obsessing, sharing our opinions.
Rather than dusting our livelihoods off a bit.
Living in the present.
Our present.
Not theirs.
Why do we focus on the kind of love they're doused in?
Only to wonder where a love like that is for us.
So many connections.
Connect us, as strangers.
Keep us intrigued, invested.
There is nowhere I go that you cannot.
Nobody cares what you're doing in life.
Nobody cares where you're going in life.
Nobody cares to support you, rarely so.
Unless they can see it for themselves, personally, too.
They have to believe, excuse me—we have to believe it's possible for us, too.
That success isn't as rare as we pretend it is.
That's why we do it.
That's why we fixate.
That's why we obsess.
What's why we imitate.
Right?

The Nerve

I don't mean for my nerves to show.
I didn't expect the audience.
I didn't think anyone was paying attention.
Funny, though.
How what we think people are looking at, they aren't.
Amazing, actually.
When someone sees you for you.
Nerves and all.
Rather than the façade we give to them in doses.
Isn't it?
He saw the nubs on my fingers where my nails used to be.
He called me out on my anxiety when so many ignored its existence.
In that moment, something was released.
There was a voice inside of me screaming.
He noticed.
He heard.
We didn't need to talk about why my nails were no longer there.
I wasn't disgusting or crazy or ugly because there were times I couldn't keep myself from hurting myself.
Because there were times I knew I shouldn't be doing what I was doing, but I kept going.
For the sake of the control it gave me.
Something else to worry about.
I didn't need to make up some excuse about why having no nails was better for me.
He saw the scars on my lips, too.
How new scabs were replacing freshly healed ones.
He still wanted to kiss me.

Told me so himself.
Told me he saw me.
But I don't think he did.
He saw how my nerves could wreck me.
He didn't see the extent.
He didn't see the why.
He thought he did such a good job at pointing out what I tried so hard to hide from even myself.
Good detective, he was.
He had nubs on his fingers, too.
I said nothing.
I guess I thought we could silently relate to each other's subtle sadness.
I wasn't ready for the wake up call he hadn't received yet.

Split

When you grow up with a split household—households if you will, you get used to a certain dynamic.
You grow up with two of every holiday.
Even your birthday.
Each event warranted a repeat affair for the sake of both parties.
Same you.
Same celebration.
Two environments.
Having two of everything becomes less of a nuisance and more of the standard.
Why doesn't everyone have two of everything like you do?
Is this better… or worse?
As you get older, branch out on your own, your events slowly consolidate into one.
For the most part.
There will always be things that you have two of.
Because you have two parents.
You have two parents with two viewpoints.
And that's okay.
And now you're in the middle.
As an adult, you are a player now.
Consciously subjecting to the games they've been playing your whole life.
Or maybe you choose not to be the middle.
Staying on the side, affected but unaffecting.
By middle, I mean the one who wants everyone together all at once.
Two of everything has always served you nice.
But now you know not everyone had that.

It's your normal but not the only way.
Being the middle is difficult when the two extremes fail to meet you.
You're stuck out there.
In the middle of nowhere.
All alone.
Nobody wants to change.
Something about fixing a thing that isn't broken.
But you never said it was broken.
You only wanted to see what one holiday was like.
As opposed to two.
See the two people you love most, in the same room.

To Be a Dandelion

I've always thought of myself as a dandelion.
It started in, let's say, high school.
The theory really set itself in motion when I would tell my tale and others would relate.
I was no longer a lone dandelion.
I wasn't the only one that felt this—whatever this was.
I was in a field of dandelions who didn't yet even identify as dandelions.
Dandelions are weeds.
Dandelions are beautiful weeds that also flower.
People pick them and make wishes.
Origin unknown, but continued practically all over.
Everyone knows to make a wish when you blow the seeds from a dandelion.
Everyone— including you.
The seeds travel and create more dandelions.
More wishes.
The wishes might not ever come true, but the story remains.
Can you see how a person could feel this way?
Like a dandelion.
A flower mistakenly called a weed time and again.
Only useful for the time it takes for some unspoken wish to become a reality.
Wishes made on a dandelion aren't usually about anything important.
But that's the magical thing about importance— it's relative.
That relativity can turn into something else relatively important.
As a person who feels they are a dandelion, they believe they are the step before.
The wish granters.
They are there to make another realize their potential.
Realize their dreams—whatever form they may take.

But the dream is not of or with the dandelion.
They are being blown upon as the wish is cultivating within the relationship that is forming.
After, when they are wished upon—unknowingly so.
Time will pass.
They will be reborn into a dandelion again, beautiful.
Their past will have moved on to something that isn't them.
And this repeats until—well.
It hasn't quite ended.

Intro II

I guess I also feel a need to give an explanation on behalf of all the broken people out there.

Even if I don't get it entirely right.
That's not the point.
But it kind of is— you know?
To not get it entirely right.

Pain is incredibly relative.
Being broken is also relative.
There's no telling if anything I say will strike a chord with anybody, but I don't consider myself an expert.

I simply want to express how it isn't always one major moment that makes you insecure for the bulk of your life or gives you a lifetime of anxiety. It isn't any one moment that leaves you covered in confusion and somehow drags the curiosity out of you. It's probably a million tiny instances that all seemed like nothing huge...alone. Snowball all of those tiny moments and you get a maladjusted adult huddled inside.

Something inside of me told me I should explain.
As if anybody could do that well.
As if nobody has ever tried.

Broken is not broken.
Broken is misinformed.
Broken is mislead.
Broken is misdirected.

This idea that a person gets one moment to define themselves for the rest of their lives has left a lot of us blaming and swapping our most vivid moments to fit into a space large enough for a collection.

That is what needs correcting.

Even now, after taking all of my own moments into account and reflecting and understanding how each one led my behavior to what it is today, I find myself in a new moment—always.

I am readjusting and growing out of old habits.
Now that I can reflect without blacking out and remember with far fewer voids in memory, I can work on that insecurity and that anxiety.

I don't need to run away from them.
I don't need to harbor them thinking things will never get better.
They can.

There are so many moments to choose from, some not even experienced yet.
Each one meant to build you, tear you down, transform you.
Snowballs aplently.

Broken is okay.
Being broken is just being unsure and being unsure is okay.

Thank you for reading.
Thank you for finishing.
Thank you for skipping to the end.
Thank you for borrowing.
Thank you for buying.
Thank you for giving me a chance.
Thank you. So much.
It means so much.

Thank you.

www.ingramcontent.com/pod-product-compliance
Lightning Source LLC
Chambersburg PA
CBHW021955290426
44108CB00012B/1078